—

Trans *For* Mission

DONNA APIDONE

Peach & Diana—
I hope to see you soon!

xo,
Donna

BALBOA
PRESS

A DIVISION OF HAY HOUSE

Balboa Press books may be ordered through booksellers or by contacting:

Balboa Press
A Division of Hay House
1663 Liberty Drive
Bloomington, IN 47403
www.balboapress.com
1 (877) 407-4847

Because of the dynamic nature of the Internet, any web addresses or
links contained in this book may have changed since publication and
may no longer be valid. The views expressed in this work are solely those
of the author and do not necessarily reflect the views of the publisher,
and the publisher hereby disclaims any responsibility for them.

The author of this book does not dispense medical advice or prescribe the use
of any technique as a form of treatment for physical, emotional, or medical
problems without the advice of a physician, either directly or indirectly. The
intent of the author is only to offer information of a general nature to help
you in your quest for emotional and spiritual well-being. In the event you use
any of the information in this book for yourself, which is your constitutional
right, the author and the publisher assume no responsibility for your actions.

Any people depicted in stock imagery provided by Thinkstock are models,
and such images are being used for illustrative purposes only.
Certain stock imagery © Thinkstock.

Printed in the United States of America.

ISBN: 978-1-4525-1814-5 (sc)
ISBN: 978-1-4525-1816-9 (hc)
ISBN: 978-1-4525-1815-2 (e)

Library of Congress Control Number: 2014912185

Balboa Press rev. date: 7/21/2014

Contents

Introduction

When I was a teenager, my head was filled with all the doubt that can come with that age. I was insecure, and I tried to be invisible so no one would notice my hair and my clothes and all the other things I thought were shortcomings. I was easily intimidated by other kids I perceived as smarter and cuter and more popular. I was sure no one liked me. I often felt I could not do anything right. In short, I was fifteen years old.

I got up early each morning to catch the school bus. In the cold winter months, I would stand in the dark at the end of the driveway and prepare to loathe the day.

On those school mornings, I was the first one awake in our house. My mother was often asleep when I left, but Dad was usually up and getting ready for work.

As I would walk out the front door, filled with dread, my father would say to me, "You can do anything you set your mind to do."

In my teenage mind, I thought, *Yeah, sure. You have no idea how it is.*

He knew. Of course he knew. He saw my potential when I could not see it for myself. He understood the power of positive thinking.

My father died just a few years later, when I was in college.

By the time I started to coach groups in the process of Transformation, I was in my forties, and I was able to see with a clarity I had not previously experienced. My dad's message, which I had not thought about since high school, came back to my mind in capital letters, with exclamation points and flashing lights.

Whether he said it to me twice or a thousand times, I do not recall. I wonder if he knew the impact of his message. Looking back, I think those few words may have been his greatest gift to me. And they are my gift to you:

You can do anything you set your mind to do.

Walking the Path

I love when my inner voice speaks to me. It is my conscience, my arbiter of wisdom and good taste. It always tells the truth, whether or not I want to hear it. My inner voice was loud and clear when I drove to the desert a few years ago, marveling at the arid landscape. The sage and mesquite gave the mountains the soft appearance of felt and velvet, with occasional points of cactus. The desert was a metaphor for my life. Everything looked soft and fuzzy on the outside, but something very sharp was trying to break through.

My trip to the desert was a retreat. I went to reflect and meditate. I thought a drive through the mountains and into the desert would calm and center me. The terrain of the Southwest is beautiful and barren. It was the perfect place to open up to all the possibilities of my life, and that is what I did. By emptying all the junk from my heart and mind, I made space for my own Transformation, and I found the voice to express it.

As a journalist, I listen and collect facts. I am an observer. My opinion is not part of the news coverage. My job is to provide information, so you can form your own opinion.

I am also trained as a life coach and interfaith minister, and I pursued those courses of study to gain a deeper understanding of people in the news. In this capacity, I am often asked to provide guidance, but again, my opinion is not necessary. Most people already know what to do. What they want from me is a little nudge in the right direction. I use the same tools as in journalism—listen and collect facts. I provide feedback by repeating, in essence, what they have told me. I hold up the mirror in which people see themselves.

TransForMission came as I reconciled my career, my training, and my passion. I searched for a way to merge all the pieces. I looked in the mirror. I found the Path. I checked the facts. I verified that what worked for me also applied to others. I listened to hundreds of people in workshops over the course of nine years, and I made adjustments as I heard their journeys. For this book, I interviewed ten people (none of whom were workshop participants) about their life-changing processes; I added notes from an inspiring memoir. The result reports the wisdom of the group. I have included my own experience when it can serve as an example of a concept.

During the time I was conducting interviews, two unrelated events added to my understanding of TransForMission.

In October 2013, Mother Antonia Brenner died at the age of eighty-six. In her first fifty years, she was Mary Clarke Brenner. She lived in Beverly Hills, married and divorced twice, and raised her eight children. At age fifty, she took vows, donned a habit, and moved into a cell in a Tijuana prison, where she ministered to inmates for more than thirty years. In 2002, Mother Antonia was quoted in the *Washington Post:*

> Pleasure depends on where you are, who you
> are with, what you are eating. Happiness is
> different. Happiness does not depend on where

you are. I live in prison. And I have not had a day of depression in 25 years. I have been upset, angry. I have been sad. But never depressed. I have a reason for my being.

Later that fall, the Make-A-Wish Foundation provided a day to remember for a five-year-old with leukemia. The boy told the foundation he wanted to be Batkid, and the foundation told the City of San Francisco. Batkid (whose real name is Miles) assisted city officials in fighting an imaginary crime on the streets of Gotham by the Bay. Batkid was joined by a lot of other superheroes that day—the mayor, the police chief, and the thousands of volunteers who cheered them on.

Some superheroes change the world without moving to a prison or wearing a mask. Cindi Harwood Rose, who lives in Texas, has found a different way to be a superhero. Cindi learned to cut silhouettes as a teen working for the Disney parks and now uses her artistic talent to raise money for cancer patients who cannot afford treatment. She explained that silhouette artists, of whom there are only a few in the world, understand how to read people. She told me the art is an image of a person's spirit, as well as his physical presence:

> To do silhouettes, one must go into the space between people and gather information as to who the person is, and that is incorporated into the work—so it is 4D ... Black and white are everything combined as well as nothing. The silhouette artwork is my magic wand into healing others and myself, as I project the

positive image from their light. That is why a
real silhouette artist does not cut from a shadow
(blocked light, the ego), and rarely should they
[work] from a photo.

As you consider how your own talents might impact the world,
you will read the comments of eleven people who asked the
same questions you are asking. They live around the United
States and in Central America. Their personalities, careers,
spiritual beliefs, and experiences are vastly different. They
have one thing in common: Trans*For*Mission. They all had
experiences that stunned them. They walked away from their
limitations. They found inspiration. They used their passions.
They found their missions.

Here are their back stories.

Dr. Richard Bruno, New Jersey
Post-polio sequelae specialist
Many polio survivors develop a second set of symptoms about
thirty-five years after their original illness. Through research
and his work as director of the Post-Polio Institute, Dr. Bruno
provides medical advice to people with post-polio sequelae
(PPS).

Susan D., Panama
The license plate says it
Susan D. is a participant in Alcoholics Anonymous and a
sponsor to others in that organization. She celebrates more
than twenty-two years of sobriety. Her license plate is
SRNITY3.

Naomi Eisenberger, New York
Former entrepreneur becomes nonprofit angel
The family retail business is not for everyone—not for Naomi Eisenberger. She had bigger plans. Naomi is director of the Good People Fund. When people want funding to carry out good deeds in the world, they go to Naomi. She raises the money and decides who will spend it.

Heather Estay, California
Life after Evan
There was no knock on the door from a uniformed officer. Instead, Heather Estay learned of her son's death in a phone call. Heather thoughtfully shares the process of looking for a reason to live after Evan was gone.

Dr. Terry Gordon, Ohio
Hay House author/Docs Who Rock
It is not a pun to say Dr. Gordon has a lot of heart. This retired cardiologist is responsible for the placement of defibrillators in schools throughout Ohio and other states. He wrote of his insights as the father of a young man paralyzed by an auto accident (*No Storm Lasts Forever*, Hay House, 2012). He co-hosts an annual fundraiser, performing in costume as various rock icons.

Jan, Washington
Solar batteries brighten Africa
After leaving a high-level corporate job, Jan went to Ghana to work on a startup company in the service sector. The business plan had all the usual goals, timelines, and financial objectives. It did not forecast that Jan would discover her capacity for love.

Jeff and Suzanna Hoye, California
Clowns at work, play, and love
Jeff, an American, was impressed with a speech by Patch Adams, the clown doctor. Suzanna, who is Dutch, saw clowning as a way to use psychology and music in medicine. They met at a clown conference in Russia. Now married, Jeff and Suzanna integrate their Way of the Clown philosophy in professional pursuits and in their relationship.

Gina Lipari, Missouri
Losing weight for charity
Some people want to lose weight; Gina was scared into it. On a trip to visit relatives, she found herself in a hospital emergency room with a clear directive from the doctor: lose weight and get a handle on your health or you will die. She was thirty-eight. Gina turned her exercise into a gift to others by walking (and later running) in fundraisers.

Captain Scotty Smiley, Washington
Blinded in combat; continues to serve
Injured by a suicide car bomber in 2005, Captain Smiley became the US Army's first active-duty blind officer and its first blind company commander. All content attributed to Scotty Smiley comes from his memoir (*Hope Unseen*, Howard Books, 2010).

Louise Vidaurri, California
From poor health to healing others
Faith healing is making a comeback, and it is no surprise to Louise Vidaurri. She turned her health around by using the practice she had grown up with. Now she guides others as they learn to heal themselves.

There Is No Time
Like the Present

New beginnings. A fresh notebook. A clean slate.

The New Year provides a time to start over. It is a holiday celebrated at different times in different cultures. Among the most commonly practiced are Chinese New Year, a two-week event that culminates in a big meal, fireworks and dragons; Rosh Hashanah, the Jewish New Year, which has a built-in act of forgiveness; and Celtic/Wiccan New Year, the eve of which is Halloween. January 1 has become a twenty-four-hour extravaganza, as we watch the calendar change hour by hour around the world. In the United States, nonprofit organizations acknowledge a new fiscal year that begins on July 1.

New Year's Day gives you a second chance. Today is the beginning of your new year.

Why Start Over?

Humans want to change. We have the wisdom to observe what we have done and the desire to do it differently. When we get off course, we see the possibility for improvement.

People ask me why I write in pencil instead of using a pen. My answer: "Because pencils have erasers." I am allowing for something better.

When we start over, we allow ourselves to improve. A clean slate represents possibility, potential, and growth. It feels good to have that window of opportunity, to have a fresh start. The celebrations are just dates on a calendar. The real opportunity for Transformation can come at any time.

There is a difference between Transformation and TransForMission.

What Is Transformation?

Transformation is not the same as change. Change is external. It may involve moving to a new address or working at a different job. Marriage and divorce, birth and death, education and employment, all involve change. These are big changes. They alter what you do.

For several years, the top-selling books were about "coping" with change and "managing" change. They told us how to tackle change, wrestle it to the ground, and control it. Ultimately, the books explained, we are in charge of change, and we can make it do what we want it to do.

That sounds like a lot of work, like moving a mountain.

Transformation is easier than change. It is internal; it is individual. Unlike change, Transformation goes to the essence of who you are. You may refer to it as the heart, or the self, or the soul, or the true being. Transformation occurs in your core. There is not a physical organ that contains your core. Doctors do not have access to it. Nor is it a thought created by the human mind. Your core is privy to the deepest level of understanding.

2

Change affects what you do. Transformation affects who you are.

Change often leads to Transformation. A near-death experience may transform you. A change in your life's work may result in a new way of being. The birth of a child changes your life forever, while the love you give as a parent transforms you.

And yet, Transformation has nothing to do with you. The process you go through has a small impact on you and a huge impact on the rest of the world. Transformation is a shared experience.

How is it possible that this core process, whether it happens in a moment or takes a lifetime, has nothing to do with you?

Connection

When Transformation happens, there is a flash of understanding in which we recognize our connection to everyone and everything around us. This hypothesis is shared in scientific and spiritual circles.

There is scientific evidence that we are connected. Those who accept the theory of evolution see an ongoing transition for flora and fauna. Humans, in our egoism, have chosen to separate ourselves from other beings, based on some kind of intellectual superiority, but evolution holds that we have been a part of the process. Perhaps we were apes who became humans. All beings have experienced some sort of growth through the ages. Only a handful of creatures are the same as they were a million years ago. The rest of us have changed.

Even at a cellular level, everything on earth is related—protons, neutrons, and electrons; energy. We are all made up of the same stuff. We are all connected.

Just as we share a scientific link, we also have a spiritual connection. Some religious teachings say that from dust to dust, we pass through this life, and as energy, we continue to be. They say our souls continue after our bodies cease to exist. If you follow that teaching, you can use your connection to reach others.

From the perspective of Transformation, there is no room for conflict. From the understanding of our connection to each other, there can only be love. Because of what we have in common, we can love each other as we love ourselves. Because of our shared core, you see something special in every person. And you can see it in yourself. As you transform, as you recognize your own value, you are lifted in greater admiration of every being.

I do not live in an unrealistic bubble of love and peace. I live in the same world as you. I work in an environment where there are goals and deadlines. I hear news reports about injustice. I hear about people who are competitive and cruel. I witness the economy and its effects on people. I have also witnessed people who keep fear and anger at a minimum, so that love can emerge as their strongest emotion.

Fitness gurus talk about "muscle memory." It is the function in which mind and body coordinate so that a person can repeatedly walk or ride a bicycle. At first, we had to learn those activities, but when we became practiced at them, we began to take those actions without a thought. Muscle memory allows us to repeat an action without consciously thinking about it. The same concept applies to fear, anger, and love. The feelings we have most often are the ones with the greatest strength. We can choose to give strength to any of them.

One of the principles of the Amish people is to "Be in the world, but not of it." While the practice is apparent in the plain clothing and transportation of the Amish, it holds a much richer meaning for all of us. We can live in and around anger and greed, but we do not have to embrace them. We can use our hearts to live beyond all that. We can choose to see there is something wonderful in each of us. We can choose to address the core of others, not what they show on the surface. We can use what is true within ourselves to reach out to what is true in others.

You do not have to take my word for it. The people whose comments fill this book have taken life events and turned them into a sense of meaning and purpose—the "reason for my being" Mother Antonia mentioned.

Connection Is the Gateway to Transformation

Transformation is not a solo art. It does not occur in a vacuum. Recognizing our interconnectedness is a prerequisite for Transformation.

In the chapter on Step 3, you will read about the benefits of connection. Everyone I interviewed found value in the support they received from people around them. Connection works in both directions. It also involves what we give to others.

We do not transform at the highest level unless we see that it is for the greatest good. To increase your income, you do work that genuinely makes you happy *and* benefits others. To find a life partner, you become the best mate in the world, an example to all who witness your relationship.

Transformation comes from deep within, but it is as much about others as it is about you. As you find your beautiful relationship with every person and thing on earth, and your connection to others, you begin to experience Transformation.

TransForMission

My understanding of mission came in a taxi in Los Angeles. From the back seat, I watched as expressionless people crossed the streets. I watched as kids unenthusiastically cooled themselves with water hoses. I was in an environment known for its creativity in music and film. Yet the air was hot and thick, and the people I saw did not look fulfilled.

Where is the inspiration? I wondered.

Inspiration comes from the Latin *in spiritu,* which translates as "the spirit within." I could have looked around Los Angeles for years without finding what I wanted. It was not there. It was in my core.

Change, combined with inspiration, leads to Transformation. Transformation, combined with purpose, leads to a mission in life.

I took a pad of paper and pencil from my bag and wrote:

Trans*For*Mission.

Without inspiration, there is no reason to make a successful change. Without passion, Transformation is empty. You have to understand your own mission in life in order to be inspired. And you have to help others to find their brilliance before you can transform.

When you are inspired, you do not just change yourself and the people around you. When you feel the full extent of your inspiration, you change the world. When you shift from thinking of yourself to serving others, you have made the first step toward TransForMission. But there is more to it than that. TransForMission is the actual shift from thinking of yourself to serving the Universe.

Wake-Up Call

In the 1990s, there was a saying—"think globally, act locally." It meant that the best way to change the world is to take action in your own neighborhood. TransForMission goes beyond that old saying. The TransForMission process relies on the ripple effect. Like a ripple in a pond, your actions go in all directions and affect people you do not know.

TransForMission comes from your passion. It depends on your interest in improving the world. Your success depends on your service. If you want to be successful for your own gain, it may be a hollow victory. If you focus your attention on making a difference to others, your success will taste sweet to you and to those who benefit.

It may be as simple as working with animals. As you studied English literature or accounting, you may not have considered how animals would fit into the picture. Some people find very creative ways to merge existing careers with other passions. Other people reach a point where it is time to finish one career and start another that allows them to focus on their passions.

A very gifted writer left her corporate public-relations job to work for an animal-rescue organization. The accountant for the same organization also left another career so she could use her expertise to help animals. These two people made a lifestyle change so they could do something they felt was important. They transformed their careers to match their personal missions.

The world had more than 1,600 billionaires in 2014, according to *Forbes* magazine (*forbes.com,* March 3, 2014). Many of them give large amounts of money to charitable organizations. Do they donate a portion of what they earn? Or do they work so that they can donate? TransForMission occurs when an individual conducts his career for the benefit of others.

All the people I interviewed recalled a moment in which they said, "What will I do with this?" They all decided to do something that would be of service to others. Look at your own work as a professional and as a volunteer and ask, "How can I best be of service to the world?" Then take it one step further, by asking, "How can I enjoy being of service?" When you are in the TransForMission zone, you are doing your best, and you enjoy your work.

In that sense, the concept of TransForMission is the opposite of "think globally, act locally." Rather than acting on a local level, you can do something that extends beyond your own circle of influence. Dream big. Be clear. You can do anything you set your mind to do.

Your inspiration becomes your mission, and your mission has the capacity to change the world. Trans*For*Mission.

What inspires you?

"Who, Me?"

You have the power to change the world.

What can one person possibly do to change the world?

When I tell people they can change the world, they look at me with doubt and surprise. Some very accomplished people have responded with, "That's a lot to ask of me!" or "Do you really I think I can?" or even "Maybe you can change the world, but I can't."

Yes, you can. You can do anything you set your mind to do.

You do not have to be Mother Teresa or Nelson Mandela to change the world. They did big things, but each big thing they did had a small beginning.

Take it one step at a time. You do not have to singlehandedly cure a disease or stop a war. Your actions and your words may be small, but their impacts can be monumental.

Start with a small impact. If you are a gardener, you are doing something of significance. Your garden may put a smile on the face of a passerby. He may go to work in a good mood because of the flowers he saw in your front yard. He may carry his good mood into a meeting, thereby influencing the rest of his team. It is a good meeting, and everyone leaves with a good feeling. Those people, in turn, do something nice. One person holds the elevator door. Someone else compliments the woman at the coffee shop.

As one smile leads to another, a small community has been affected. Most of them do not know you. Most have never seen your garden. They just know they had a good day. And it all started with one person who liked the scent and the palette of the flowers you planted in your front yard.

If you can change so many lives with a few flowers, imagine what else you can do.

When you do your absolute best, it *does* change the world.

"A" Students

What kind of grades are you getting in the classroom of life? Even if you only do "C work" for yourself, you can work a little harder to get an A when it comes to doing good things for others.

We can make the world a better place. That was the theme of the late 1960s and early 1970s. Music, art, and politics all called for love and togetherness. The youth of that era believed they could change the world. More than that, they believed it was their responsibility to do so. The sentiment faded for a few generations before re-emerging in the 1990s as a wave of volunteerism. After the millennium, faced with terrorism and huge natural disasters, people once again showed their generosity by sharing their time, energy, and finances.

We cannot stand still. There is much to be done. We are called to action, and our efforts will earn an A for ourselves and for those we serve.

That's what Trans*For*Mission is all about.

The Trans*For*Mission Path

The following chapters lay out the Five Steps of the Trans*For*Mission Path. When you read them, you will see that you are just five easy steps away from transforming your life in a way that changes the world.

The Trans*For*Mission Path is a helix, like a spiral staircase. Each of the five steps has its own lessons and exercises. When you finish all five steps, you are at the next level, where you can begin the process again, just as you repeat the circle from one flight to the next on a staircase. Ever higher.

Every step of the way, you will see yourself and others in a new light. That light becomes brighter as you go. The joy, exuberance, and fulfillment you feel as you walk this path will spread to others.

The Trans*For*Mission Path

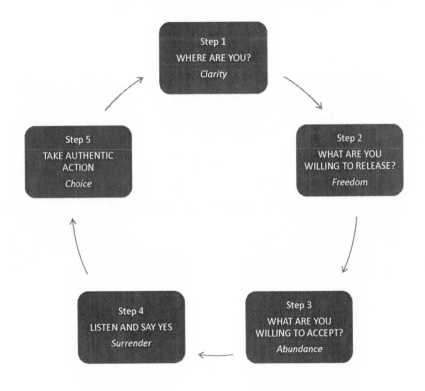

STEP 1

Where Are You?

In order to move forward, you must know where you are.

The foundation of this step is Clarity.

There was a dust storm in the desert, as wide and as high as I could see. It was more than a cloud of sand; it was a tan wall, slowly moving through Death Valley, and it was headed my way. I took cover in a cantina, one of the few buildings in a hundred-mile radius. From that little diner, I watched as high winds blew and sand darkened the sky. Visibility was reduced to fifty feet. The wind rattled the restaurant, and the electricity went off.

The dust storm lasted for several hours, making its way across the desert floor like a blizzard of sand. After it had passed, I set out to explore rock formations in the area. With the distant, dark tan storm as a backdrop, the colorful rocks glowed in the emerging sun. The contrast of light and dark made the colors more vivid and clear than they seemed just a few hours before.

The wind must have sandblasted my mind too, because I saw how easy life can be. My life started to shine like the brightly colored rocks. My darkness had blown away. I clearly saw how all the pieces of my life fit together. They were all visible to me for the first time. Step 1 was underway.

Step 1 is about clarity. It is about being truthful with yourself.

Look Closely

It takes a lot of courage to look very closely and see the truth about yourself, especially in the middle of a storm. The people I interviewed identified an unexpected, life-changing moment of clarity—an injury, a death, a change in career, a change in perception. They can recall the incident as if it has just happened. And nothing is the same. That moment forced them to look at who they were.

Explore your core values, thoughts, emotions, and reactions to others. See who you really are. Have you ever said to someone, "You don't know me very well"? Get to know yourself. You have more than one persona. The person you want to be, and the person who others think you are, may not be the real you.

For example, if asked to explore the color red, you might protest, saying, "We all know what red looks like." As you explore, you become aware of the subtleties of red—the orangey version, the dark shade with a hint of blue, the brass and the deep wine used as hair color, the basic crayon that matches Christmas ornaments and flags—and you would see that different shades of red fit in different settings. You would start to notice how red is used in décor, in sports cars, and in clothing. Whatever your opinion of the color, you would gain a deeper, fuller understanding of red.

So it is in the process of TransForMission. Look at the subtleties of who you are. Become aware of what you do and how you do it. You will see how your actions and reactions serve you in some situations and not in others.

Spend some time on it. Even if you know yourself very well, you will see your life in a new way because you are looking through the lens of TransForMission. You have the opportunity here to review your standard thoughts and comments. The things you have done over the years can be improved.

Start with your core values. What is important to you? Your core values shape the way you think and the way you live. They are the essence of who you are.

In the upcoming pages, Gina mentions broken relationships within her family, yet family is one of her core values. Is it one of yours? Why? Is it because you want to tell people how great your kid is, or is it because you can share with a child lessons that will be passed on through the generations? Do you want your family to be well known in the community, or do you appreciate the precious, private moments between loved ones? Do you have a traditional family, or do you create a family with others who share your values?

Several interviewees identified with their professional status. When careers shifted, they felt a loss. Look at your career. Is work a core value for you? This book was inspired, in part, by a person who told me, "You are not your job." I had identified so closely with my career that I had to explore its importance in my life. I discovered how much I love my job, and I also discovered how I could move forward if my job were no longer a part of my life.

If work is one of your core values, look at the reasons. You may use the income to acquire a lot of luxuries or to pay for your children's education. Or you may place a high value on your work because you consider it your mission and you are passionate about it.

What else is on your list of core values? You might include compassion, generosity, humor, integrity, creative expression, and respect. You might expand your list to include the creation of beauty in all your surroundings, or you may focus on making sure technical and mechanical gadgets are working well.

Look at what is important to you, and look at why it is important. Your core values may need a touchup from time to time, but for the most part, they will last you a lifetime.

Next, explore your attitude. How do you interact with others? Do people see you as friendly and compassionate, or do they find you bitter and angry? Do others welcome you into their conversations, or do they stop talking when you walk into the room? Do you cry a lot or crack jokes about everything that happens? Acknowledgment of your attitude will lead you toward a clearer understanding of who you are.

In quantum physics, there is a debate over whether an observer changes a situation just by observing it. By observing your emotions and by understanding yourself, you can move beyond where you are. Your TransForMission depends on it.

Discover yourself. Find clarity. This is a time to explore and get to know yourself in a new and deeper way. You do not have to make any changes right now. Your TransForMission will come as you make your way up the spiral staircase.

Here and Now

In Step 1, we become comfortable with ourselves where we are. It is a lesson in *now,* living in the moment. This is not a time for looking back or forward. You cannot change the past, and the future is not yet known, so start here.

When you are in the present, you have no one to blame, no regrets, and no fear of what might happen. It is as easy as saying your name. Who are you? Where are you? You are right here, right now.

Who are your heroes? Who are the people you admire? You might select a world leader or a person who has brought peace to the world or someone who accomplished great things with very few resources.

How did you learn about your hero? Did you read an article or watch a biographical profile? Chances are you found out everything you could so you could emulate that person's wisdom and actions.

Discovering your hero shapes the way you live. Yet your hero is much more than his back story or accomplishments. The person you admire has a core. If I were to ask you why you admire your hero, you might give me some highlights of his life, but you would not repeat every detail. You would focus on one or two nuggets that made an impression on you.

Yet when I ask people, "Where are you?" I often get a detailed life history. Your background shapes you, as it did your hero, but you are not your history. You do not have to live in the past. It does not serve you. It is over. In order to live fully, in order to transform, focus on where you are now.

The future can be a land of promise and opportunity, or it can be a black hole of excessive planning. Devoting time and energy to hopes and goals can be an escape that slows your progress. Planning becomes the activity. Instead of taking action, we devote ourselves to the plan. Nothing happens. When we hide in our hopes for the future, we rob ourselves of the joy of living in the now.

Statements such as "I wish I could be more ..." and "I'd like to be able to ..." are common in our society. They give us something to look forward to. There is a fine line between looking to the future and missing out on the present.

When clarity comes, you do not look back or toward the future. Heather describes her physical reaction to the news of her son's death. The reality of the moment was so powerful, she fell to the ground.

People who have had near-death experiences say they have learned to live in the moment. They understand what is important. It is not success or fame (their pasts), nor is it their striving for more (their futures). Those who have knocked at death's door say the lesson is to be completely present, to focus on what they have, and to live in full appreciation.

Our histories and our goals shape us, but they are not who we are. There is something bigger within us. Your core, your essence, is what allows you to shape yourself. Your history and your hopes for the future are just a small part. The process of TransForMission allows you to move beyond who you think you are, to become who you really are.

In Step 1, you discover who you are. You see where you are. TransForMission is coming to the understanding that what you did or who you know or how much you have is not important. TransForMission is the discovery of who you really are.

Take your time with your exploration. Savor it. If you discover something that surprises you, do not dwell on it. Just acknowledge it and continue to explore.

Say What?

The way you express yourself affects your TransForMission. If you are visiting Paris for a short time, you can speak English and get by just fine. But if you want to live in Paris, it is better that you immerse yourself in French.

The power of language is an important element of Step 2, and we get a taste of it here in Step 1. Positive language leads to positive thinking, and that, in turn, leads to positive action. Negative language just leads to more negativity. Whether you look at your life in positive or negative terms is a choice—*your* choice. You can decide how you want to live by your selection of words.

By saying, "I hate my job," or "I always end up in relationships with jerks," you confirm that thought, and you continue to live that way. You stay stagnant instead of moving forward to something better.

It is worth your time and effort to find a positive way to express your situation. Negative talk keeps you at a standstill. Positive language propels you. With positive language comes the freedom to change.

As Susan says, "It has to be intentional." Put the power of positive language to work. Ask yourself, "Where am I?" Let the answers inspire you. Instead of saying, "I'm stuck," or "I hate my job," you will see your potential. "I'm ready for a new career." "I'm going to do something new."

You can turn the bad things in your life into a fresh view of what can be. You can do anything you set your mind to do.

Here in Step 1, you do not have to know all the answers. You have to answer just one question: Where Are You? As you uncover the answer, the pieces of your life will fall into place. By putting your time and energy into this first Step, the rest of the TransForMission Path will be an exciting journey of discovery.

So that is Step 1: Where Are You?

Walking the Path to Clarity

Gina: I went to visit cousins in Ohio in 2009, and I got very sick while I was there. I had excessive swelling in my ankles, feet, and legs, and they turned a horrid shade of purple. When the ER doctor leaned over my bed and said, "Only ninety-year-old people get things like this," it was then that something clicked in my mind. I had to do something about my weight and my health, or I wasn't going to live.

Susan: I was desperate, and I had no more answers, and I had no more choices. Desperate was, "Why am I doing the same things over and over again? Why am I never getting results? Here I am in the same spot. Nothing ever changes. And I need help, because I can't do it anymore." I was alone. I didn't know what to do.

Heather: What happened was, he was in L.A. He was working to be a filmmaker... They didn't have an address, so they called. The LAPD... It was in the afternoon. It was like everything shut down... I went into a fetal position... Just knowing at that point in time you're entering a new reality... And it was a totally, like, crazed feeling of just so much pain and very few words.

Suzanna: I was already going through some sort of Transformation. I had spent most of my life in some form of cult, being very suppressed and told what to do and what to think and how to live. At some point, we had to move away. We had to get away from one of those groups.

Richard: One day, I got a call [from a polio survivor who had been misdiagnosed with Lou Gehrig's disease]. The poor guy is calling around and asks me, "Well, have you done any studies to know how long I have to live?" He didn't have Lou Gehrig's disease. He was our first post-polio patient, and this was in 1982. So that's how it started.

Louise: I got up one morning, and I could barely walk down the stairs. I couldn't eat. I was too tired to chew. I heard the words come to me, saying, "If you don't quit doing this, you're going to die." And that was a turning point for me. I knew that day I had to give up my career and choose differently, or I wasn't going to live.

Terry: I think I was being prepared for this. For probably decades, this transformational enlightenment was slapping me in the face. I just didn't realize it. People started coming into my path at just the right moment. And yet, I hadn't gotten to the place where I accepted that.

Jan: I was approached by someone I had worked with before, who had a business idea and needed a partner. [He] really believed that economic development was the secret sauce to help the developing world advance.

Naomi: More than twenty-two years ago, I met someone who was an incredible inspiration to me ... a man who went around the country looking for good people... I heard him speak. I was just blown away by the people he was describing.

Jeff: It was an accident. I wound up dressing as a clown and flying from Denver, Colorado, to Moscow, Russia. I had the garment, and I had no idea what I was supposed to do or how I was supposed to act. It was only in Russia, and after bumbling around with this group associated with Patch Adams, that I started to get what it was.

Scotty: Surgeons at the American military hospital in Balad moved rapidly to save my life and mitigate the long-term impact of my traumatic brain injury. The shrapnel stuck in my left frontal lobe had placed my life in peril, but the swiftness of my evacuation from the battlefield lowered the danger level from grave to worrisome. A multi-hour operation that removed the metal from my brain and repaired my damaged dura mater (a thin but tough layer just underneath the bone of the skull) also left my brain badly swollen.

Suzanna: I was more aware [than Jeff] already, before I got into the whole thing, that my life needed some major change. It was this—I didn't see how. Before I was in Russia, I thought the only way to change my life was to end it.

Heather: Evan lived on the edge, so it was a drug overdose. It wasn't suicide, and he was responsible. He took that kind of chance.

Terry: And there was this one guy. He said, "Well, I see all this energy around you. It's all great energy, but it's fractured and fragmented. You really had better do something about it or something very bad is going to happen to you."

Gina: I weighed 325 pounds approximately. I was completely sedentary, inactive. I had high blood pressure.

Jeff: It snuck up on me. I'd like to say that, yeah, I really had to step through a scary doorway or some such thing, but it wasn't that.

Scotty: "For better or for worse" once meant that I sometimes came home grumpy. Those five words would soon take Tiffany somewhere altogether unimagined.

Gina: My relationships with my daughter Emma and my father were broken. I was single. My mother and I still managed to get along at that point and I had been completely focused on my genealogical research.

Richard: Post-polio sequelae is, literally, the sequel to having had polio... Because the brain-stem damage is now being revealed over time as both simple aging and attrition of these neurons due to their overuse is causing them to pay a price.

Scotty: I had experienced significant brain trauma—trauma that might have altered my personality.

Terry: What he suggested to me was that I open my eyes. Not just to see what was right in front of me, but to really open my eyes. And the challenge he gave me was to be open to everything—attached to nothing—and I'd never been that way before.

Scotty: The bond of marriage turns two into one. My blindness suddenly became her blindness. The next fifty-five years of my life became the next fifty-five years of hers.

Richard: The more polio survivors I met, the more I realized that they were totally different in terms of the way that the polio virus affected them. They were individuals who had had virtually no muscle weakness or paralysis at all to individuals—one of them who could only move the pinkie on her left hand. So physically, they were all different. Psychologically, they were identical. They were all Type A—hard-driven, pressured, time-conscious, overachieving.

Gina: [I was] depressed. But on the other hand, I was so driven by my genealogical research that I kept in close touch with cousins and family.

Naomi: About six years ago, he came to me and said, "I'm retiring, and I don't want this organization to continue." And I felt like somebody had just pulled out the rug from underneath me. I was depressed, overwhelmed that this incredible experience was being taken away from me.

Heather: I have a very strong feeling that we all have our path, and this was Evan's... He had his own determination.

Jeff: [Patch Adams's] subject was healing health, and I will tell you this: I totally fell in love with him and who he was and what he was doing in the world. I felt something, listening to him. I felt something I hadn't felt before, and I was really moved by this human being, and I'd never met anyone like that—to read about them, but to actually meet. This is for real. I had to know more about him. I was more than just drawn—compelled—to go over there.

Richard: By 1995, we knew exactly what was happening. This had nothing to do with the polio virus. This was just the central nervous system disintegrating as a result of overuse/abuse.

Terry: I've always been a very happy person. I've never been at peace, even though I'm happy. There is a distinction.

Gina: I went directly to Weight Watchers and started the program. I was driven. I believe the thought of death and the reality of my situation gave me fear as a motivator I had not had before.

Terry: Everybody is different. Everybody comes into an experience with a different template preceding the experience... We're all unique individuals. We're all unique spirits and souls. None of us has ever had an exact duplicate, because we've had different experiences. Everybody goes into it differently. A lot of it is attitude.

Scotty: Blindness makes the simplest of tasks adventurous. I can't read a restaurant bill or even sign my name in the right spot without help.

Suzanna: In the Netherlands, where I lived, they have a bunch of clowns that go into hospitals to clown for sick children. I see these clowns going through the hallway in the hospital, and I know that's it. I want to do that... I always try to be very present with people. That's what the Clown is all about... It's all about stepping into a different reality. And I'm trying to practice that without a nose on.

Heather: It's a continuous process. I'm not sure I have come up with an identity or a role to follow what that one was.

Susan: It has to be intentional first. That is basically the whole thing, right there. It has to be intentional to take those steps.

Suzanna: To be where I am, connected with whatever happens in that moment. It's my spiritual practice.

Implementing Step 1: Where Are You?

In order to move forward, you must know where you are.

The foundation of this step is Clarity.

- Where are you? Express your situation in one sentence, without reference to past or future. Focus on what is happening now.

- Learn to speak "Nowese." It is a language that has only a present tense.

- Become fully engaged.

- What gives you juice? What is your passion? What gives you energy? What lights you up? What would you rather do than anything else?

- What is clear to you?

- Do you believe we are all connected? If so, how do you honor your connection with others? If not, consider your belief on the topic.

- What is your purpose in life?

- How do you honor the journey you have just begun?

- What are you most grateful for in Step 1?

STEP 2

What Are You Willing to Release?

You select the people in your life and the actions you take.

The foundation of this step is Freedom.

The wagon trains came into Death Valley, and they found they could not get out. The weather was hot and dry, and the wagons were not built for the desert or for the rugged terrain of the steep Sierra Nevada range that was ahead of them. Many of the pioneers had to leave the Valley on foot, carrying only food and water. They left behind most of what they owned and held dear. Walking away from belongings and family treasures may have seemed like a loss, but it was the only way these courageous people could reach their destination.

To prepare for a new way of living, you have the opportunity to discard what is no longer useful to you. Just as you remove old food from the refrigerator or donate clothes you no longer wear, Step 2 allows you to release anything that is stale or does not fit.

Throughout our lives, we collect items and people and behaviors, and we get used to having them around. We become attached to them. We think we need them.

The truth is that I do not need the contents of my garage. I do not need all the clothes my closet, nor do I need all my books and gadgets. I like them, and I use them, but I do not need them. They will not go away on their own. I have to make a conscious effort to dispose of them.

The same is true of some of the people I know. I do not need them. That also goes for situations. There are some I should dispose of. They will not go away on their own. As with the boxes in my garage, I have to sort through and get rid of some of them.

Step 2 is much bigger than getting rid of people and things that drag you down. Each of these people and things is a reflection of a choice you made. In the process of discarding what is no longer useful, this step gives you the freedom to dispose of the action behind your choices.

Most importantly, you have to be willing to stop accumulating unnecessary things and people, and you have to be true to that effort.

Willingness is a commitment of the highest order. The word *willing* has confused some people. They say, "I'm willing, but I just can't seem to do it." If that is the case, they are not truly willing. They may want it, and they may think it is a good idea. When we are willing to do a thing, we do it.

Before you look at your relationships, focus on your lifelong habits. Explore the decisions and actions that brought you to this point, and acknowledge that you allowed those things to happen. Some people find it hard to admit to making choices that did not go well.

Rather than look at it as something that is hard to do, view it as something that is easy and joyous; by making better choices, you are now allowing wonderful things to happen. Extrapolate. Although some of your choices were bad, you have already made many good choices, and you continue to do so, which means good things are happening now and will continue to happen.

Sometimes we "give up" things we like. This was the case when I was a kid and we gave up something for Lent. We considered it a sacrifice. In Step 2, you are giving up something that is not helping you. It is not a sacrifice to give it up. It is a joyous release. This step sets you free.

Terry had to release the control he felt as a doctor. Jeff gave up what he had perceived as a perfect life. Jan and Louise lost their incomes. Everyone felt grief over a lost identity. The freedom came in surviving the loss.

What are you willing to give up? What will you eliminate from your life routine? What habit or action are you ready to release?

Here is a more positive way to frame the same question: What is one thing you can let go of that will allow you to be free? Are you willing to release any habits or routines that do not contribute to your TransForMission? Look closely.

Remap Your Route

If I told you that on my way to work every day, I drive through a thick, dark swamp, where I encounter dangerous, wild animals that block the road and jump on my car, what would you say? You might suggest I take a different route to work.

Step 2 is about finding a path that is lighter and brighter than the road you have been traveling. It allows you to release old habits. It allows you to observe your routines and change them.

We value truth from others, but we find it convenient to hide our own truth behind stories and routines. They seem normal, because we have repeated them so many times, but they do not advance our Trans*For*Mission.

I often ask myself this question: "Really, honey?" It is my loving, gentle way of examining what I say, think, and do. I ask myself for the truth. Are my words taking me forward? Am I telling a story that gives me an excuse? Am I acting in love and kindness? Am I at my best?

Those two words—"Really, honey?"—serve as my barometer for the truth. They remind me of what is important to me. They help me to measure who I am in my core.

What do you see when you look at your habits? Is there something you want to release? How would it benefit you? Do you see how the habit has held you back? Are you willing to give it up? Really, honey?

Be sure to release these negative forces in love, not in anger. If you dismiss them but retain your frustration with the person or the situation, then you have not really let go.

The Power of Words

Step 2 is about letting go. As you release what no longer works, you can release negative language from your vocabulary. Words like *stuck*, *struggle*, *difficult*, and *hate* do not advance your TransForMission.

Terry says, "I changed the paradigm of thought in a nanosecond." That is all it takes. In an instant, you can change your words and your thoughts and benefit from the adjustment.

Words have power. The metaphysical Law of Mind Action holds that "Thoughts held in mind produce after their kind." If you say you are struggling, you will continue to struggle. If you say your situation is difficult, it will continue to be so.

You can use the power of words to your advantage by releasing language that does not contribute to your TransForMission. At first, observe how you speak. Remember the quantum theory of observation, in which you alter the situation just by looking at it? It applies here as you release negative language. Listen. What words are you using? Do they motivate you, or do they hold you back?

As you continue to observe the language you use, you will discover new words to replace the old. Let your thoughts and speech be filled with promise and potential, and you will start to see your direction. It is really that simple. When "I'm stuck" is replaced with "I'd like a new career," the sentence often becomes augmented with more detail. "I'd like a new career ... that lets me spend more time with my family"; "... that involves working with animals"; "... that has flexible hours."

In just one sentence, with a shift from negative to positive language, you have seen what works for you and what does not. "I already knew I wanted to work with animals," one person said. "Then why haven't you done it?" I asked. The word *stuck* was such a big part of her lexicon that she had overlooked what she already knew.

People You Do Not Need

Feng shui is the ancient practice of arranging space to maximize the flow of positive energy. One component of feng shui, often used in home décor, brings peace and serenity into the home by removing clutter. A cactus near your front door might prevent good people and good energy from entering your home. A foyer cluttered with shoes and coats and a week's worth of mail would also prevent the flow of positive energy. The practical interpretation is that guests do not want to scrape their arms on the cactus or trip over the shoes that were left on the floor. It makes sense that good people are staying away.

The people in your life are part of your spiritual and psychic décor. The non-supportive people are the cactus and the pile of shoes. Their presence at your front door limits the number of supportive people who will come into your life.

Just as you release words and habits in this process, you can release people who do not contribute to your TransForMission.

Who is around you? Look carefully at your relationships with people at work, in your family, and in your social circle. Do they enrich you, or do they defeat you? Do they add to your life, or do they deplete your energy?

In an earlier chapter, you saw the connections of all beings in science and in Spirit. Releasing people from your life requires great courage and compassion on your part. It takes courage because you may have to tell someone that you are on a different path. It takes compassion because you recognize your connection to the person you are releasing. Release them with love, because everyone deserves love.

Why is it important to clear these people and events from your consciousness? There are several reasons. The first reason is that they take up valuable space in your mind and in your heart. When you buy a new car, do you keep the old one? If there is a reason to keep it, you might. But if it no longer runs well or if it is not something you want, you will probably sell it or donate it. It is the same with some of the people and memories in your life. If they are not working, get rid of them. If they have value, commit yourself to reviving and refreshing your relationship with them.

Gina says she released a couple of people until she dealt with the emotions she had about them. She later reconsidered those relationships.

You will not feel a renewed commitment to everyone you know. You may choose to release some people permanently. Releasing a person from your life does not suggest hatred for them. To the contrary, it indicates your love for yourself and for the life you are designing through TransForMission. Some of the people you release in Step 2 have been nothing but trouble, and you never want to see them again. Others may have played an important part in your life, and you may be sad to see them go, even if you know it is for the best. Love them, but from a distance.

Do not let emotions cause you to hold on to someone who is not living with your welfare in mind. Be truthful with yourself. If you know in your heart that the person is detrimental to your TransForMission, let him go.

It goes both ways. Just as you release people who do not support your TransForMission, you may find that others are releasing you. This is the natural flow of life. People come and go. Your new way of thinking and being may look unusual to some of your friends and family. They may think you are acting "weird" or they may say you are being "pushy" as you express your discoveries. They do not mean to insult you; they are noting the changes they see in you. Listen to what they have to say. Learn from them. Love them. Honor their requests to be free of you.

Release Judgment of Yourself and Others

Judging others is an act of ego. When we judge others, it is an attempt to make ourselves better than them. Sometimes we judge others on a characteristic we do not like in ourselves. We judge because we do not want to admit that we have so much in common with others.

As you release other people, you have the opportunity to forgive them. Forgiveness is a major element in your growth and TransForMission.

Forgiving others allows you to be free. Forgiveness does not condone their behaviors. It simply means you are ready and willing to move forward, to leave the past in the past.

If you have judged yourself, you can stop now. As Louise says, "I was disappointed ... but guess what? You let go."

Louis Proto offered a forgiveness exercise in his book, *Self Healing: Use Your Mind to Heal Your Body* (Berkley Books, 1991, 107). The person you forgive need not be present. The forgiveness occurs in you. Proto called it "Letting Go of Grief" Visualisation:

> See the person or scenes from the relationship over which you have been grieving too long. Allow yourself to really feel the pain of loss. Where in your body do you feel the hurt? Try to isolate the components of what you are feeling ... is there anger there? Some guilt perhaps? How exactly were things left unfinished between you? What wasn't said that needed to be said? See yourself saying these things now to the person. Be absolutely

honest and speak from the heart. Pause for a while and listen to the other's response. What is their message to you? Allow yourself to feel whatever you are feeling—and give yourself plenty of space for this ... Stay with whatever comes up (however unexpected) until you feel "finished." Then, as gently and as lovingly as you can, say goodbye.

Forgiveness is an integral part of Step 2. There are a lot of theories about how to forgive. One of my coaches says if you do it right, you should only have to forgive once. On the other hand, a teacher named Jesus suggested you forgive "seventy times seven" times (Matthew 18:21–22). Some people say they can forgive the little stuff on the first try, but bigger offenses require a bigger effort. It does not matter how long it takes.

So that is Step 2: What Are You Willing to Release?

Walking the Path to Freedom

Scotty: I didn't believe God still loved me, and I was certain I could do almost nothing at all.

Terry: Most doctors feel like we are in control. We're not. We're just the tool. We're just the conduit, but we're not in control.

Susan: I knew I had to get down to basics, and it was the only way I was going to succeed.

Jan: I left a very good job by all of the measures society uses to decide whether a job is good.

Jeff: One of the things I realized was the scorecard I was using, which is an acceptable scorecard, was no longer the right scorecard for me.

Heather: Besides missing him, [I was] missing who I had figured out I was going to be.

Jeff: Remember those snow globes you see around Christmas? Pick up me in my snow globe, and just turn it upside down, and shake it and set it down. It just flipped me upside down and turned me around. I was totally not ready for what happened. I don't know if I would have gone if I had known.

Suzanna: In order to become a clown, I had to just be me. That's where my globe was turned upside down. Me—who is that?

Scotty: I don't want pity, but just close your eyes for an hour and sit in your living room. It gets boring pretty quick.

Louise: That day, I called my [boss] and said, "I can't come to work anymore." And I called my husband, which was really hard, and I said, "I can't work. I have to stop today." There was dead silence on the other end, and I thought, *Crap. I'm letting a lot of people down.*

Jan: The biggest thing I had to get comfortable with was releasing having an income... I had never in my adult life been reliant on another person's income. I was contributing nothing to the mortgage, to the bills... Yeah, it was a big deal.

Susan: I was willing to risk being poor and homeless—in my mind, that's what was going to happen to me—with the hope of change. I was willing to risk everything in the hope of something better. That's really quite a freedom.

Richard: There was tremendous misinformation and tremendous discrimination against these individuals... [A patient said,] "Normal wasn't good enough. We had to be better than normal. We had to be better than everybody else just to break even." That's why these folks were so Type-A, are still so Type-A.

Naomi: I think people who serve others receive an unbelievable gift. It's a privilege, in my mind, to be able to do that. The trick is being able to do it and not destroy yourself at the same time, because you have to be able to step away a bit ...

Gina: There is freedom in forgiveness. During my weight-loss journey, I became estranged from my mother and daughter completely. So I was on my own and focused my entire attention and energy on saving my own life.

Louise: I had to let go of the life I had known, what I had done for twenty-five years, which had become my identity. Who would I be without that?

Heather: The cataclysms I've had in my life—a lot of it is identity. So early on, I had to recognize I'm no longer Evan's mother. I'm not going to have grandchildren, at least not my own grandkids. All these things that get taken away. It's an identity that gets taken away. So, for me, the marker points are: Okay, who am I now? I'm not that, so, okay, who am I? And who am I going to be? And stepping into something different because my identity as Evan's mom was really strong.

Jan: My passion is in problem-solving, figuring things out, building things where there isn't anything already. I really thrive in project work and startups, and what I really came to realize is that large corporations, at least at that time, were not where I was likely to find a lot of personal satisfaction.

Richard: It turned out that these [polio survivors] were overachievers. And over the course of time, overachieving caused them to pay a price. Had they been laid-back, they probably would not have developed PPS or developed the symptoms to the extent that they have them today.

Scotty: I resented the theft of my dreams—my hopes of becoming a Fortune 500 CEO or a Delta Force operator or a four-star general. Instead I was a grown man who needed help walking across the street.

Terry: As a scientist, we generally think in a certain way. We believe only what we can actually visualize. And that changed for me ... and it was dramatic.

Gina: I had to forgive myself for not being this over-exaggerated image of a blonde rock-groupie type that was a size two, and completely accept myself for who I am. "I am Gina Lipari, I have a curvy body type that is ethnic, real, and appealing to men, and I must appreciate the attributes I do have and let go of the things I don't." I remember I used to cry when I was a teenager all the time that I wanted to be pretty instead of smart. I had to let this attitude and mindset go because I carried that with me until I was thirty-eight years old.

Scotty: Blindness had altered more than just my ability to see. I often lost track of time—minutes and hours, even days and weeks. I could remember events, but something about the lack of sight made it difficult for me to put those events in chronological order. All of my memories were now auditory.

Suzanna: There is a big difference between me and my persona and the Clown. I wish there wasn't. I'm not a clown authentically. I sometimes feel I need to do things that others expect from me. But the Clown doesn't have that at all. As the Clown, I'm fearless.

Scotty: My words came from a place of fear. Not only did I fear that God had abandoned me or had never been there in the first place; I feared that I would soon be just some sympathy piece to my wife. These feelings of despair and insecurity fought for ownership of my heart. After years of optimism, they were my new reality.

Terry: It is ego. When we first embarked on this path—our family—it was very tumultuous ... I had in my mind, as a physician and father, what we should be doing and the timeline that we should be doing it. And every step of the way, there was resistance. And it wasn't until I let go of the ego—completely—and realized that this is not my journey. This is my son's journey. This is his path. It's his potential learning experience. It's not mine—although I am learning in parallel—but it's his journey, and they are his decisions to make, not mine.

Gina: I had to accept that I would have to leave my father behind. He has been absent for the majority of my life, and when he has been present, he says things that are so hurtful that I cannot move forward. I had been a victim of a sexual assault at age nineteen, and that is when my life changed. I ballooned over the years in size, until one day I was over 325. I had to forgive myself for the rape, because I felt that I had been responsible for that in some strange fashion. So leaving my father and stepfather behind were key in my ability to lose weight.

Jeff: It's really strange to be in the middle of what you thought was a game, and you're playing, and you're winning, and you suddenly realize, "Oh my goodness, that doesn't work on a couple different levels for me right now."

Suzanna: That was never asked of me. I was always asked to conform.

Terry: I changed the paradigm of thought in a nanosecond, and I went from "I'll believe it when I see it," to "I'll see it when I believe it." And that, perhaps, was the greatest Transformation in my life, because it was a totally different path that I was embarking on in doing that. And, as a scientist, that's a difficult thing to let go of.

Gina: I moved to Riverside, away from the inner city. Away from all the reminders of my life from that time.

Suzanna: Once I made the decision, I had the courage and the strength to have all the difficult conversations.

Richard: With regard to all of the symptoms—the fatigue, muscle weakness, trouble swallowing, muscle pain, joint pain, all of those symptoms—if you take the Type A away, those symptoms either decrease or go away. That's absolutely true.

Heather: One thing about it: there is very little that can scare me now. That was the scariest thing that could ever happen, and it happened, and there is nothing that can scare me now. I guess that's part of my new identity. So it's a kind of freedom.

Terry: Most of us, you know, we're attached to our belief systems. We're attached to our experiences, to whatever it is. But he taught me to not necessarily accept what he said as truth, but at least to consider the possibility. And it set me off on this totally, totally different path.

Scotty: Daily life has its difficulties. I can survive without being able to see a basketball game. What hurts beyond measure is not being able to see the people that I love—never being able to see Tiffany again. I feel her face. I feel her hair. I picture what she looks like, but I start to forget. People are always telling me how beautiful my son, Grady, is. Sometimes I even get jealous when others see my kids for the first time and get to rejoice in that. It's hard on me. It hurts so much that I try not to go there.

Heather: I've always honored grieving. I need to let it have its place. But it can't just take up your whole life.

Suzanna: I felt like I had the permission to just look for who I was, and that made me cry. I was miserable. And then I knew. I couldn't live like that anymore. And because I started crying, I was really encouraged to go to all those feelings, and to what I really wanted and what I really felt, and it just opened up everything. And there was no way back. Absolutely no way back.

Louise: I was disappointed that I couldn't produce the income ... but guess what? You let go.

Naomi: I, myself, have found this to be very freeing: You don't have to do it all. It isn't going to all happen at one time, first of all; and it's okay if it doesn't all happen. That's very freeing.

Jeff: It doesn't matter if I'm doing strategic planning with a leadership group or we're looking at some large-scale change in an organization. In order for the change to occur, it happens at the personal level, and most people are afraid to change. If I let go, if I change, I'm going to have to give up... It doesn't matter if it's a CEO or the staff out on the floor, helping see the change, see the need for the change, but then being fine with the change. I can let them know it's going to be weird, or you're going to resist it, and when that happens, it's okay.

Implementing Step 2: What Are You Willing to Release?

You select the people in your life and the actions you take.

The foundation of this step is Freedom.

- Release three people who do not support your Trans*For*Mission. You do not have to tell them you are releasing them. Just release yourself from their holds.

- Forgive five people. You know who they are. To let them know you have forgiven them may stir up old conversations and emotions, and that is why you are letting go. Forgive them in your own mind and in your own heart. Release them.

- Ask forgiveness from one person. This action frees you from judging yourself.

- Find one place in your home or office that can be cleaned or cleared. It may be a corner of your desk or a kitchen cabinet. Clean it. Clear it. Next week, do another.

- Release three things from your home or your work environment. There are three things that are taking up space. Observe how you are lighter and freer after you release them.

- Release one habit. It may be a word or an attitude that does not contribute to your Trans*For*Mission. Conduct a little ceremony to send that old habit on its way.

- Add two words to your daily practice: "Really, honey?"

- What are you most grateful for in Step 2?

What Are You Willing to Accept?

Life is filled with people and things that will aid you in your TransForMission.

The foundation of this step is Abundance.

The tiny species called pupfish have adapted to their desert environments. They swim in water with a high saline level that would kill other fish in minutes. Likewise, desert rodents thrive against all odds. They have learned to absorb relief from the heat in their underground burrows. The desert is filled with amazing creatures, large and small, that have learned to live in hot, dry conditions.

As humans, we are amazed at the capacity of animals, and even of early humans, to live in an arid landscape. Neither the pupfish nor the cactus nor the indigenous peoples made an effort to conquer the dry air and lack of water. Their success in surviving through the ages stemmed from their willingness to accept their surroundings.

The flora and the fauna did not "struggle" with the desert. They did not try to change it. They were not in conflict with the environment. Rather than defy nature, they transformed to live comfortably in the desert. They made the most of what was around them.

How can you accept what is all around you and make the most of it? How can you fully enjoy the abundance of your own environment? How can you use it to serve others?

Having released people, habits, and language that did not serve you in Step 2, you can now bring into your life new experiences to support your TransForMission. In Step 3, you accept and embrace the best in your life. You see the best in others because you accept the best in yourself. You see everyone as a source of love because you see yourself as love. You are more accepting of yourself when you see how you are a part of others.

You can begin by making a list. Maybe you can keep it all in your head, but there is a reason to write it all down.

Make a Buddy List. Who are your buddies? Who are the people you can trust to support your TransForMission? They may already be within your circle, or you may not have met them yet. When you are open to TransForMission, the right people seem to appear out of nowhere.

Heather learned it takes a village to mourn a child, just as to raise one: "I don't know that I really cultivated [a support network] before, but I'm so much more aware."

When you make your list, you are celebrating your abundance. By abundance, I do not mean material wealth. I am talking about the people who make your life enjoyable. Pay tribute to the wonderful folks who teach you, inspire you, support you and believe in you. Make a list of all the people who have made the world a brighter place for you. If you have ever been grateful to someone, write down that person's name.

Step 3 asks that you ascertain the good things in your life, but it suggests more than that. It would be very easy to rush through your Buddy List. By taking great care and by spending time on this step of the Path, you can develop a greater appreciation for all that is available to you.

Somewhere along the line, the word *accept* received an interpretation that is aligned with resignation, as in, "I guess I just have to accept that." For the purposes of TransForMission, the word *accept* does not mean "to make do." The word is associated with joy. It is synonymous with "embrace."

You can embrace and joyfully accept all you have in your life. All of it.

Although Step 3 is the opportunity to expand your buddy system, the list is not limited to people. You can also add some other resources. For example, you might give recognition to your talent and wisdom. Louise welcomed knowledge she had not put to use. This is a loving action, in which you can wholeheartedly accept the good people and things around you. All statements are expressed in a positive tone. When you come to something you do not like, stop until you can see the good in it and then write it down as something you embrace.

Here are some examples. Say them and see which ones feel like a good fit:

I accept:

- that I am surrounded by love.

- that I am where I need to be.

- my power, my talent, my love, and all I give and receive.

- that I am successful because I trust.

- my Trans*For*Mission.

- that I find the answers when I inquire within.

- help, from Spirit and from my earthly connections.

- my wisdom.

- that I can trust myself to act, speak, and *be*.

- that I am open and generous.

- the confidence to be humble.

- that people around me believe in me and support my efforts.

- all that has brought me to this point.

- that everything in my life is good.

This sampling of the many good things in your life also serves as a sort of Buddy List. These are the resources you can turn to when you need a boost in the process of your Trans*For*Mission.

All these good things and more are already in your life. Look closely. You may be surprised to find all the goodness that surrounds you.

Attract the Best

In the introduction to this book, I revealed the most important element of TransForMission—believing in oneself. In my dad's words, "You can do anything you set your mind to do." My father was teaching me the metaphysical Law of Attraction, which says that we attract what we think about and give energy to.

As kids, many of us were taught, "You are what you eat." By eating strong, healthy foods, we grow to be strong and healthy. Conversely, by eating junk food, sugar, and fat, we grow into unhealthy adults.

The Law of Attraction teaches an equivalent. It says, "You get what you think." This is your opportunity to replace your unproductive language, released in Step 2, with words that advance your TransForMission. Starting now, you can use positive, supportive, and encouraging words. This applies to what you say to others and to the encouragement you give yourself.

Like any new habit, this takes some practice. Be gentle with yourself as you take on this new habit. Look at it with the excitement of learning a new language. It is not Italian or Polish—it is Transformese. Adopt words that reflect where you are going in your TransForMission. Verbs, or actions words, are your best bet—*create, teach, build,* and *invent* are a few examples. These words reflect what you are doing for others in the world. They define your activities while they explain how you share your gifts and talents with others.

We draw toward us that which we think about and say. What a wonderful discovery! We are what we think, so it is easy to attract a new way of being.

As with the Law of Attraction, express your desires as if they already exist. Try these on for size:

I accept:

- that I have the funds to attend courses and get my degree.

- that I can earn (fill in a number) dollars as my salary.

- that I am a loving partner in a loving relationship.

The Law of Attraction says that you attract what you think about, so you may as well think about what you really want.

This step is not complete until you have expressed gratitude for all the wonderful resources of your life—those that exist now and those that are taking shape. Every one of these buddies and resources is dear to you. Be mindful of their presences in your abundant life.

Identifying your resources is more than a casual activity. The people and talents you identify are your lifeline to a new way of being. You can call on them for support. You can reach out to them for answers. You can count on them. If you could not, they would not be on your list. Love them, be open to them, and let them help you.

This is called a Buddy List because it holds valuable resources that help you move toward your mission in life. Inanimate objects can also serve a purpose in your TransForMission. Buddies can be the kind who give you a hug or the kind that sit on a shelf. Is there a book that guides you or motivates you? Add it to the list. How about a place where you can retreat, as I did in the desert, to renew your spirit? Write it down. And while you are at it, write down the things you say and do for yourself as a boost to your morale. If you benefit from looking in the mirror and saying, "You can do this. I know you can," then add "mirror" to your list. If you sit with a cup of tea to refresh yourself, then add "tea" to your list.

Now that you have made your list, double it. Does that seem an unusual request? After all, you have written down all the people you could think of who might be resources for you as you move forward. One man put his dog on the list, as a source of unconditional love. And now you have to expand the list? Imagine that.

Yes, that is how you do it. Imagine it. Who can help you? Who can you call on for answers? After my list was filled with the names of friends, coworkers, and family, I challenged myself to double it. I wrote down the name of that nice guy at the post office who always has good ideas about shipping. I added a friend who is an attorney. He knows all the other good attorneys in town and can help me get an appointment. I wrote down the woman who runs the dry-cleaning business at the corner, because she knows a lot of local businesspeople. I also added my boss to the list, because each of us wants the other to be successful. I added my dogs too.

I was not finished yet! I added some organizations to my list. I promised I would donate 10 percent of any new income I generate, so I added to my list the nonprofit groups that will benefit from my success. By putting them on my list of resources, I engaged them as my buddies. They became my partners in success. And they do not even know me.

That is a key point in developing your Buddy List. Whether it is your spouse or the guy at the post office, each buddy is a partner in your success. Maybe you can get by without them, but we are all more successful if we work on a successful team. So add them to your list, even if they do not know they are on it.

Add me to your list. I want you to succeed.

So that is Step 3: What Are You Willing to Accept?

Walking the Path to Abundance

Suzanna: I wanted to help other people. That's why I first thought about studying psychology. But I also wanted to be playful. I wanted that to be my passion.

Naomi: This is just very exciting. This is just the most exciting thing I could be doing. Who—other than an obstetrician, who is delivering babies all day long—who else gets to do just good things all day?

Susan: I was ready to listen to someone other than me. I became open that there might, in fact, be someone—it, he, she—out there helping me. And then, as I went along, it was proven to me.

Gina: I define success [as] being blessed with beautiful grandchildren, an amazing boyfriend who wants me to be the best me I can be. My mother and I have a working relationship and work together in the best interest of [my grandson], and I have extended family all over the world who care for me.

Naomi: It's having someone who knows what you're going through and that [you're] not alone. It's what allows [you] to take that step.

Jan: It felt to me like such an imposition on them to have a houseguest for the weekend, so for the longest time I would make up the kinds of polite excuses we would make up here. Finally, they just put their foot down and said, "You're coming... Your concept of imposition doesn't exist in Ghana."

Susan: My mind is a bad neighborhood, and I try never to go in there alone.

Jeff: It's pretty special. As with most things we all do in terms of volunteering, the secret we all learn pretty quick is, "Wow, I get so much more out of that than the person I was helping. I thought I was there to help, and it turns out it was really all about what I was needing.

Naomi: I know I always get more out of it. There isn't any question in my mind that I get way more out of it than what I give.

Louise: I have an abundant life. I have wonderful friends. I have wonderful opportunities. I help people every day. That's a big reward.

Jan: I have a larger capacity for embracing others in my life than I realized.

Gina: I encourage anyone I see struggling with the problems being overweight presents. Once I saw a cashier in [a store], and she was well over three hundred pounds. She talked to the customer in front of me about why she couldn't exercise, her health problems, etc. So for some odd reason I took it upon myself to tell her the cashier how I knew how she felt and how I had done it... I just didn't feel right leaving her without at least sharing my story.

Scotty: Ocean [the new dog] became a quick friend, and while training her to go to the bathroom outside didn't involved the tactical, interpersonal, or cultural complexity of leading a platoon in Iraq, it did give me something to do. There is no doubt that I needed Ocean.

Naomi: You want to look for people who share your passion, and that's always the nugget I give them. Find people who share your passion because they will work hardest for you... Sharing the passion is the most critical piece.

Jan: It definitely was my family away from home, and that was not something I could ever have anticipated, feeling as connected to them as I did. They were really true adult friends.

Louise: There's a peace that comes with that. Abundance of mind and abundance of what I send out into the world, because if we're sending out [abundance] into the world, we bring it back to us.

Naomi: The moral support is a very, very big piece of what we do, and it's recognized. There are grantees who say the mentoring and the moral support is as important as the monetary support.

Susan: What they say is, "You alone can do it, but you can't do it alone." So whatever that is, I have to know that I'm not alone.

Naomi: I think this country is a generous country, and that most of the people in it are generous, and as their ability to be generous increases, they will be. People want to give, and people want to help, and I think that's very much a part of who we are in this country. I really believe that will continue.

Louise: It takes time for people to accept, just like it took me time to say, "I have to be who I am in the world."

Suzanna: We didn't speak any Russian, but the clown has a universal language, and we were able to connect and be so appreciative and so touched.

Jeff: It touches something in me, and I found that when I went [to Russia] too. And I've had that happen only a couple times in my life up until then.

Suzanna: I wanted to do something with a group where the need was bigger. And I thought, *All these elderly homes that are filled with people who are basically tossed out of society and end of story. I want to go there...* So we called our colleagues together that were interested and started an organization that specifically works with people in elderly homes.

Heather: I spend a lot of time alone. But being *all* alone? Wow.

Jan: I believe in love, and I believe in relationships with other people. So while I was glad I had the experience of starting a business in Africa—I learned a lot of business lessons and learned about a lot more functional areas of running a business than I had known before—on the business side, I don't think there was a time when I said, "Oh, wow, I'm so glad I did this." There wasn't what I would call a revelatory moment. On the other hand, I did have that moment around many of the people I met there.

Gina: Encouraging words mainly about how I looked or how was I doing it. I began writing a blog, and people also loved commenting on how the blog helped motivate them.

Scotty: Mary Lynn never had a specific moment of Transformation, but over the course of three days, my little sister evolved into my protector. Her entire identity shifted from vagabond tourist to my personal concierge. Every ounce of her energy had gone into my emotional care. She says it was like a mission—she would not leave my side.

Terry: For me, I think the most profound thing that I have learned is to accept that everything is in perfect order, that there are no mistakes, there are no accidents. And I mean *everything* is in perfect order.

Louise: I had the knowledge, but I had to put the knowledge into practice.

Naomi: I think most people will know when they've found that person. Something clicks... Those are the kind of people you want to draw in.

Gina: I really believe resources and people showed up as needed. When I first started, I didn't have money to join Jazzercise or a gym, so I went to the park every day to walk. Being in nature and having the ability to feel close to God helped me many times to sort out many of my feelings.

Scotty: She was an ultra-loving dog. When I walked in the door, I could hear her wagging tail slapping against the closet door. Even if I had been gone for just a few minutes, Ocean was happy to see me.

Gina: I gathered a lot of support from my coworkers who cheered me on, I went to regular meetings at Weight Watchers, so the encouragement continued. I also got a lot of support from fellow Jazzercisers. I had a personal trainer for a while, and she was very helpful in helping me to realize I wasn't weak, that I had strength, ability, value, and worth.

Heather: I can't imagine going through something like this without a support network. I think a lot of us think we have one until the shit hits the fan. I don't know that I really cultivated one before, but I'm so much more aware.

Louise: I knew there was no way I could do it by myself. That was my prayer: I know I can't heal myself, but I know there are answers for me to heal myself... Show me, and I will do it.

Susan: I can love myself exactly the way I am, faults and all. It doesn't matter. It's just about genuinely caring about others and yourself.

Implementing Step 3: What Are You Willing to Accept?

Life is filled with people and things that will aid you in your TransForMission.

The foundation of this step is Abundance.

- Make a list of your buddies. Whether or not you know them well, write down the names of people who support your TransForMission.

- Make a list of your resources. Include your education, your computer, your sales techniques, your compassion, and your natural talents.

- Thank five people who have been supportive of you. Call them or visit in person. Let them know you noticed their support and appreciate it.

- See yourself as others see you. Ask three trusted friends to tell what they most admire about you. You are not just asking for a compliment; you are getting a better sense of what is in your core. That is what others see in you.

- Imagine a group of people standing at your front door. They are there to work with you in your TransForMission. You can decide who will enter and who is turned away. Only those who support your efforts can come in. Who are they?

- How do these people and resources increase your abundance?

- What are you most grateful for in Step 3?

STEP 4

Open the Space— Listen and Say Yes

What you are seeking has already been given.

The foundation of this step is Surrender.

Three of us were working on an archaeological dig that afternoon. It had rained a lot during the days prior, but at this time, the Arizona sky was bright blue. There was a crashing noise. We climbed the ladder out of the top-entry pueblo to find out what made the noise.

"It's the dam," Jim said. Indigenous peoples had built the dam hundreds of years ago to have a supply of precious water in this desolate landscape.

"Look at that," he said. I did not know what I was looking for. I heard it before I saw it. We heard a low, long, thunderous noise—the sound of rushing water. As we watched from above, the water gushed its way down a creek bed that had been dry too long. It was a beautiful sight, a mix of grace and force.

A few days later, the creek bed was dry again, but it was lined with the bright green of new plant life inspired by the water.

We hiked up to the old dam. No longer a reservoir, it was now a half-empty crater. Its internal walls exposed bones of long-dead animals. And here, too, new plants emerged.

When the dirt walls of the old dam broke, there was nothing we could do to stop the flow of rushing water. We had to stand back and watch it carve its path. It was nature's way.

The dam's gift to the Native Americans was a supply of water. To the three of us, it gave flora and dinosaur relics. Those bones were not removed from the desert. We left them there as evidence of the event, as the dam surrendered to nature.

Listen

An ancient text (Ecclesiastes 4:6) says, "Better is a handful of rest than a double handful of hard work and striving after the wind."

This is the time for rest and reflection.

Step 4 is the rinse cycle. You went through a cleansing phase as you released and then accepted in previous steps. This step allows you to cogitate, to ruminate, and to pay attention to what you have uncovered. The most remarkable thing about this step is that it does not require a deliberate effort on your part. You do not have to think or do anything.

Only one thing is asked of you: Step 4 asks you to surrender.

"Step into the open space," Jeff says, "because that's where life is."

Something bigger than you is speaking. It happens all the time. It may be your connection to the Universal Grid, or it may be your own highest internal knowledge. There is something in your core that knows and understands more than you consciously recognize. In Step 4, you acknowledge the information is available, and you allow yourself to hear it. The message has always been there. Your mind and your heart are now open enough to hear.

We tend to interfere with our own higher understanding. We block it and tune it out with more mundane and superficial thoughts and sounds. Science tells us the human mind cannot successfully multitask without missing something. If you drive a car, talk on the phone, listen to music, and discipline your kids in the back seat, you take your mind off the action of driving and compromise the safety of those in and near your car.

Worse yet, we analyze our understanding. In trying to figure it out and explain it, we risk distorting the message as it was given.

Our thoughts and activities also distract us from hearing the small, still voice within each of us. It is not until we dismiss the distractions and really get quiet that we can hear what we need to know.

In this context, *surrender* means we clear our heads of thoughts and distractions, so we can hear what is coming into our hearts and into our connected core. That is where we find our answers. We can tap into this knowledge through stillness and meditation.

Meditation can be an easy skill to learn. There is no special equipment to buy or special place to go or fee to pay. All you need for meditation is a quiet place and about fifteen minutes. If you have access to an experienced teacher, go for a lesson in person. If not, you can learn on your own.

In a Huffington Post article (*huffingtonpost.com*, March 15, 2013), Massachusetts yoga master David Magone outlines five steps to meditation:

1. Set an alarm clock to help keep track of the time. Begin with three minutes, and work up to five.
2. Find a comfortable, seated position (feel free to sit in a chair if you're not comfortable on the floor).
3. Sit up tall, rest your hands in your lap and close your eyes. Your palms can face up or down. Simply choose the one that feels the best.
4. Take a few moments to relax and settle in. If any part of your body feels uncomfortable, mindfully shift to a new position.
5. Once you feel relatively comfortable, redirect your mind to your breath and begin counting your exhales. Set an initial goal of counting a total of 21 and build up to 108 with practice. When your mind wanders, refocus by drawing awareness back to your breath, and begin the count again.

As you get close to your core, you will be amazed at what you hear and see during meditation. With time, practice, and consistency, you achieve a calm, clear understanding.

Our minds fill us with distractions that make us tired and confused. Meditation clears the fog and lets you see and hear with greater focus. As you continue your meditation practice, you will discover increased energy and focus, because that is what is growing in your core. Experienced practitioners can tap into meditation anywhere, even on a busy subway.

There is no predicting how much quiet time will be needed for you to know what is within you. Each person is different. There is no hurry. Your patience pays rich dividends.

The experienced meditator does not have to ask, "What did I get from that session?" She simply knows more coming out of the meditation than she knew going in. Answers become apparent. Whether it is the same hour or the next day or a week later, you will clearly see what to do. And you will recognize it is not a thought born of logic or consideration. It is knowledge that comes from your connection with your core and your connection with all others.

What do you hear? What is "occurring" to you? Whether you get it in pictures or in phrases or in grammatically correct sentences, this is the information you have been waiting for.

Write it down. Even if it does not make sense to you or you are not sure of it, make some notes as these thoughts come to you. The only thing worse than not hearing what is inside you is hearing it and ignoring it. By taking the time to write down your discoveries, you can connect the dots of this knowledge at a later date.

Many times, I heard a clear message but ignored it. I would fervently hope for an answer or solution. When I would get it, I would say, "Nah, that can't be right," and then continue on in my ignorance. I heard the answer, and I rejected it. That string of errors led to my understanding of Step 4.

Some of us have to learn to surrender. It was not natural for me. I was born fighting and thinking my life was unfair. I had to learn to be still before I could listen. I had heard enough of my own voice. It was time to hear what the Universe had to say. The Universe, Nature, Spirit, God or Goddess—whatever name you give it, it is the force that gives water the power to create and destroy. It speaks to each of us.

I had to stop fighting before I could hear what the Universe had to say. That was the purpose of my trip to the desert. It was a way to stand in the stillness with nothing around.

Then what?

Nothing. Wait.

Sometimes, the only thing I heard was the wind. Fifty-mile-per-hour winds whipped through the desert for several days, whistling through fig trees and scrub pine.

Farther into the desert, where there was no vegetation and nothing to offer resistance, the wind made no noise at all. We think we "hear" the wind, but we are hearing the trees and buildings as they fight against it.

I am the same way. When I fight against the Universe, I make a lot of noise. When I offer no resistance, the Universe and I do our work together quietly.

I was in the middle of nowhere, in an expanse of sand and sage and mesquite, and there was no sound at all.

Silence. TransForMission is in that silence.

When I became as quiet as the wind, the answers were clear. When my mind was devoid of thoughts and clutter, I heard what really mattered.

Simple messages are all around you. The dog waiting by the back door is a message to let him out. Mold under your sink is a message to clean. The red light at the side of your car's fuel gauge means the gas tank is empty. You do not have to be highly intuitive to grasp those clear messages.

Expand your hearing and vision to recognize more subtle signs and messages. If you get a headache when you talk with your neighbor, it is a message. If your boss does not like the work you do or takes credit for your work, that is a message.

Listen to the messages. Adjust your situation. When you think you have done all you can, listen again. Maybe there is more.

Say Yes

Listening to your inner voice through meditation is only the first half of Step 4. The second half involves heartily accepting what you hear. It is one thing to slow down in body and mind to listen to the voice within. It is quite another thing to say yes.

Yes is open and unconditional. It is not, "Yes, but only if ..." or "Yes, and another thing ..."

Yes is a complete sentence: Yes. Period.

Saying yes is a courageous action. Trust that the answer is real and right. In Susan's experience, "I don't know anything. I just trust. I'll get what I need to know."

Surrender. Close your eyes and take a deep breath. As you exhale, eliminate all the thoughts that start with "But ..."

Instead, say yes.

You may think you know better than the voice of your heart. You may judge what you hear, or you may second-guess it. That is the difference between thinking on the surface and having inner knowledge. If you find yourself unsure of which is which, continue with the meditation portion of this step. Ask yourself what is coming from the mind and what is coming into your core. With practice, you will discern the difference.

Saying yes changes everything. The more you trust the information in your core, the more willing you will be to say yes. Say yes to things you never thought you would. When you look at starting a new career, your inner voice will make it clear what you should do. When you wonder about investments and consider personal relationships, you will know what to do. The answers may surprise you. You may not always understand what you are hearing. Say yes anyway.

Once you listen and hear your inner voice and say yes, all the details fall into place. Instead of creating chaos by fighting what is right in front of you, you can "go with the flow" and feel peace and joy. Instead of fighting, bucking the system, and insisting you know best, you can enjoy the abundance the Universe has to offer. With your agreement, by saying yes, you will notice the right people show up, the right situations arise, and you are successful in what you do.

Richard says, "It's certainly a lot less work and a lot more relaxing to say, 'This is me.'"

Surrender is the dam when it breaks. When that old soil breaks away, there is nothing left to do or say. Just stand back and let the water flow. The truth will find its way to you.

You can say yes to everything the Universe has to offer. All it takes is some practice, an open mind, and an open heart. Start by saying yes to the easy things, such as a detour on your way to the park.

Every time you say yes, it gets easier.

So that is Step 4: Open the Space—Listen and Say Yes.

Walking the Path to Surrender

Terry: The thing that was starting to happen was the more I opened up, the more stuff came in, and the more opportunities there were to say, "Oh, that's what this is about." And it happens all the time.

Scotty: It was a truth that my blindness was going to help me see. My confidence was being moved away from self—from my own ability to see and control—to a new hope, a hope unseen.

Richard: Surrender is the most important and the most difficult step for polio survivors to take, because they are terrified. They are terrified that what happened to them when they were three, five, seven, ten years old is going to happen to them again... They will be discarded, as they were discarded when they were young.

Jeff: Suzanna knew the Transformation and power, so this – what we call the Way of the Clown—one of the tenets is you just say yes. Step into the unknown, and step into the empty space, because that's where life is. It happens there, not in our head or in some other way. As soon as we get out of our own way and step into what wants to be said or done. And that takes a lot.

Suzanna: It's that kind of yes. You step into the open space without expectation, without thinking about what the other possible outcomes would be, and you say yes to what happens. And you see, and you go with it where it wants to go.

Scotty: Parking lots were a blind man's outer space. No up, no down. No left, no right. Just an empty wasteland of concrete that could quickly induce massive disorientation.

Susan: It's a knowing that, in spite of everything that's going on, everything's fine.

Gina: I meditate on walks; I listen to my thoughts in a race; I listen to the voice of God telling me that I can do this.

Heather: There are some things that are kind of bubbling up, that are moving forward, but I'm still listening.

Naomi: [Holocaust survivors] are teaching us stamina, fortitude, that goodness can prevail over evil without any question.

Jan: When I say I believe in love and I believe in relationships with other people, the "aha" moments for me connect somehow with other people who are perhaps very different from me, but not entirely different.

Jeff: Wouldn't it be great if we could live in this space of everything is yes? There is no censoring, but it's all the right thing to do. Because the yes comes from that place.

Naomi: Sometimes I can't even put it into words. I'll look at a particular prospective new program, and I won't be able to verbalize why I think it's a good idea, but in my gut and in my heart, I know this is going to work. And I'm always right.

Terry: I embrace that we're presented with potential learning lessons all the time, and we have the free will to decide whether or not we're going to learn from them. If we don't learn from them, we'll be presented the lesson again and again and again, until we get it right.

Heather: There is something that is mine to do... It's finding that.

Susan: I don't know anything. I just trust. The wisdom is in not knowing. And when I need to know something, I'll know when I need to know that. I'll get what I need to know.

Louise: On a spiritual level, we know who we are. Our highest self knows who we are, but we are always trying to be what we think other people want us to be. And that was a big deal for me. That was the hardest part for me, coming out and telling people who I really am: I am a faith healer. I went into meditation and said, "No matter how embarrassed I am, help me to tell people who I am. Please help me."

Scotty [his italics]: *God, what do you want from me? Why am I here? How am I supposed to wake up every day and live like this?*

Louise: The best choice [to get where I am today] was to say yes to my spiritual direction. There was no other choice. Am I going to die? Or say yes?

Heather: There was something in me that had to say, "This is precious." Feeling it, and allowing it to move through me.

Richard: The terror of what happened to them when they were children, and even young adults, teenagers, and they have to surrender the terror. They have to surrender the fear. They have to, in a sense, be naked to the world and say, "Yeah. Here. Look at me. I had polio."

Naomi: I frankly didn't know what I was going to do, and then I just said, "I'll start over!" ... There was no question in my mind that this was what I needed to do, and I was going to make it happen, come hell or high water.

Scotty: In difficult moments, I could look back and encourage myself that God really did seem to be guiding our lives. That He did have a plan. That He loved us and had not forgotten us.

Terry: If you allow something to unfold as it is going to unfold, whether you like it or not, you learn valuable lessons in observing it happen. I had to sit there and be patient and wait for it to unfold at just the right moment. And for me, a lot of that has happened when I'm outside in nature... It had to do with patiently sitting under a tree and just being and experiencing and watching and observing.

Richard: The model for retirement, I think, would be the polio survivor who surrenders, who go from their "work lives," in quotes, of being "normal" and Type-A, and surrendering and retires to become who they really are, which is a polio survivor... It's certainly a lot less work and a lot more relaxing to say, "This is me."

Louise: I *do* live in a sea of unlimited possibilities. I don't know if it's going to come from here or here or here, but I don't have to know. I just have to show up.

Suzanna: It's all about being authentic and saying yes to whatever. The clown always says yes. People feel accepted, and they open up. So it proved itself to be a perfect match—the clown and the elderly person, especially people with dementia or Alzheimer's.

Heather: When you are in the presence of death, that veil between life and death is thin. It was way thin... It's really kind of beautiful.

Susan: [My sponsor] Harvey said it real clearly. He said that every now and then, just for a test, he'd wake up in the morning, and he'd decide he was going to say "yes" to everything that happened that day. So if somebody said, "Harvey, I'm going to go get some tools at Home Depot, you want to go?" "Yes." No matter what it was. Whatever needed to be done, he would do it. He would not say "no" to anything.

Richard: What happens when polio survivors surrender is that they are less Type-A. They will allow themselves to use a crutch, return [to] the brace they had, or get a better and a newer, lightweight brace. Use a wheelchair when they need to, park in the handicapped parking space. And they feel better, almost immediately. The first thing that goes away is pain, and then fatigue, and then weakness, and then their symptoms don't progress.

Gina: To give in, to be free to let go of the pain, accept who I am and where I came from and move forward to the life I was meant to live.

Susan: [When I say yes,] I have a new adventure. I have a new experience. I get to know somebody a little bit better because I took the time.

Louise: The thing is just me opening up and saying yes—yes to Spirit—not matter what I think ... just letting go.

Terry: Those things continue to happen. They're miraculous—I really believe that—but you have to be receptive to them... It's divinely orchestrated, but you have to have the antenna up to be able to perceive it.

Implementing Step 4: Open the Space—Listen and Say Yes

What you are seeking has already been given.

The foundation of this step is Surrender.

- Find a meditation teacher. Even if you already meditate, a guide may help you improve your practice. Learn to achieve stillness.

- Recall five times when something popped into your consciousness. You do not have to know what it means. For now, just recognize that a message has been given.

- Investigate the spiritual practice of surrender. It means different things in different belief systems. Find out which version rings true for you.

- When have you said yes to what the Universe has offered? Were you ever surprised by your response? How did you know yes was the right answer?

- The next time you are tempted to say no, stop. Change your response, and see what happens.

- What are you most grateful for in Step 4?

STEP 5

Take Authentic Action

You can only plan it for so long. Then it is time to do it.

The foundation of this step is Choice.

The coyote circled two tourists walking their Chihuahuas. *Easy prey*, he thought. But there was one thing Coyote had not counted on. He had not counted on me. I called out to the humans to warn them of the predator. They hurriedly picked up their bite-sized dogs and retreated to their car. Coyote put his ears back and snarled at me. He knew he had waited too long.

Coyote and I each made a choice. One of us took authentic action, and the other did not. One of us went away satisfied with the outcome of the event. The other one went away hungry.

By now you know where you are. In the first four steps of the TransForMission Path, you rallied your resources. You eliminated damaging habits and influences. You heard in the wind the direction that is intended for you. Now it is time to take authentic action. This is your time to shine.

An authentic action is one that is grounded in truth and reality. It is clear and decisive. It feels right, even if it is unpopular. It is an action you take for the greater good. It is the right thing to do.

What will you do? What will be your authentic action? Will you go away satisfied—or hungry?

Authentic action is an inspired choice. Such an action is rewarding because it is an act of love. No one can tell you what your authentic action should be. Even if you work with a coach or count on a mentor, it is up to you to determine what action you will take and when. From there, a coach or spiritual leader or friend might agree to encourage you to complete your action and will celebrate with you when you have done it. The action is yours for the taking.

In Step 5, your efforts and your mission become one. This is when you know what you have to do. You know how it will take shape. You are ready. Most of the people I interviewed mentioned their passions and responsibilities. They talked about life's magical aspects and about making contributions. And they all recognized they had made what Scotty called, "the choice to keep going."

Each time I travel the TransForMission Path, I complete a few authentic actions. In doing so, I have found there are two kinds of authentic action—simple and complex.

The Book—A Simple Authentic Action

The book I wrote as an authentic action is not the book you are reading now. It is the workbook for the TransForMission workshop.

After teaching the workshop for several years, I had developed a lot of written materials to give to participants, and it was no longer practical to have a pile of handouts. I thought it would be a quick and easy action to merge the separate computer files into one and give it a cover page. That was when the word *authentic* kicked in.

To be true to the workshop and to participants, I could not simply throw together a workbook based on exercises I had accumulated in the past. The effort deserved more devotion. I rewrote exercises, did some research, studied page layout, and rearranged the order of the pages. When I had carefully reworked all the pages and put together a cohesive workbook, my action was authentic.

Restoring Integrity—A Complex Authentic Action

The restoration of one's integrity is an authentic action. In my case, it was a series of actions. I had been aware for some time that I was not living in integrity. I had used the TransForMission Path to explore and to determine how to proceed. By the time I reached Step 5, I saw my options.

I could blame other people for my unhappiness, or I could take action. I could insist I was right, or I could take action. I could refuse to cooperate, or I could take action. I could quit a job that fit my talents, or I could take action.

The authentic action I chose to take was to bring integrity to work with me. It is not the job, but how I do it. A job description is a piece of paper that does not have integrity. It is up to the person who holds the job to keep her integrity in the work.

In the complex authentic action of restoring my integrity at work, I developed an intention and a question. My intention is to be the creator of a supportive work environment. My question is, *How can I give the love I want to receive?*

Within every authentic action is the opportunity for TransForMission. Like the garden that changed the world, every authentic action comes from the heart. Your action may have a direct impact on just one person, but the ripple affects the world.

Do not concern yourself with the magnitude of your authentic action. Just take it.

Step 5 Leads to Step 1

After you have taken authentic action, simple or complex, it is time for an evaluation, one that allows you to begin the process again as you reach for the next level of TransForMission.

An objective look allows you to see the magnificence of your work, and it allows you to consider what you might do differently the next time around.

The word *evaluation* might scare a person who had a bad experience in school or at work. The process is not frightening or difficult. All you have to do is explore. A regular evaluation process is *de rigueur* in a lot of industries. Imagine the opportunity to look in the mirror and redesign your path every week or every month!

Step 5 gives you a clear view of your work so far. By setting a clear checklist or set of criteria, you can track your progress. You can review your work independently, or you can ask for input from a trusted friend or colleague who can provide an unbiased perspective.

The evaluation is not the end. It is the beginning. It informs you of your progress. Evaluation tells you whether you have met your goals. The evaluation process helps you remain focused and headed in the right direction.

You have the opportunity to continue the process or to make a fresh start. As you climb the spiral staircase, you advance your TransForMission.

The Path is not without its surprises. Every now and then, you will find that a step has rotted out, and you do not have solid footing on which you can place your full weight. You will decide whether to step gingerly on the edge of that next step or skip it and make the big stretch to the secure step above it.

Some steps may have wet paint. Someone has come to your staircase and painted the steps without telling you. That is how it is on the Path. People do things you are not expecting, and you have to maneuver around them. You learn to step around that guy with the paintbrush, to avoid getting paint on yourself.

Look how far you have come! When you stood at the base of this wonderful spiral staircase, you groaned with despair and cried in confusion. You did not know how to move forward. You could not imagine making progress.

Yet here you are. You have already climbed a full flight of stairs, just by taking one step at a time. The next flight will be easier, and the one after that will be even easier.

"And it always gets paid forward," Naomi says. "That is the beauty of it all."

So that is Step 5: Take Authentic Action. And prepare for the next adventure.

Walking the Path to Choice

Jeff: The whole journey of Transformation is knowing what to do, but it's not from my head. It comes from a different place.

Suzanna: Starting a nonprofit always takes a lot of effort, getting together, making plans. But most of all, you need to go and do it.

Heather: Sometimes Transformation gets kind of thrust on you, and you have the choice to go for it and be open to it or not. So, yes, this whole process has been very transformational.

Terry: My firm belief is everything is in divine order, so when something happens that doesn't make us happy, that doesn't bring us pleasure, that causes us heartache, it's not a tragedy unless I decide to make it so. The real tragedy is in going through something like this and not learning from it. Even if it's a small lesson, it's purposeful.

Louise: Your perception has to change if you want to change. You have to see life differently for life to be different. And then it happens. I really believe that. Whatever my perception is, that's what runs my life. But if I change my perception, that new perception will change my life.

Heather: It doesn't matter what the decision is, but to see it as conscious... Recognize that you made a decision, and this is what you want. It's not something you have to do.

Terry: The Kabbalah—which is an ancient mystical text of Judaism—in it, it says it's the falls of our life that provide us the energy to propel us onto a higher path. Those falls in our life don't really seem that magical, but they can magically transform your life. And it's really not the cushy, good things in life that cause us to transform. It's the other stuff. But they're all magical.

Jeff: It's the Way of the Clown. It really is about transforming lives one at a time. That's the level that change happens.

Susan: Love. I care more about myself.

Gina: My weight loss was a conscious effort. I had the realization that I was worth saving.

Heather: Now you have to face, "Are you sticking around for you?" You don't *have* to stick around. I am going to stick around for me.

Suzanna: I think it's very important how we come into this world and the way we leave this world. Life should be celebrated as much. When I was in Russia, I saw all these children—orphans—being close to the most cruel things, and it was just heartbreaking. And I thought, *Now, these kids, they don't really have a choice. But I do.* All of a sudden, I realized I had a choice, that I could change my life. And that's what I decided to do, because I knew it was this or … it was "do or die."

Gina: I realized I could live my very best life and that I was worthy of a healthy body. I didn't have to be a size two. I just had to be healthy so that I could do things I had dreamed of.

Richard: Oh, I can't stop ... I can't leave these people. I will die at my desk typing to a polio survivor. I'm the only one left. We've studied, evaluated, and treated about six thousand polio survivors. These are individuals I know, names I know. At this point, with the Internet, in the United States, Canada, and now China, India, Pakistan, Africa, South America—there are people who are e-mailing me and getting on the Facebook post-polio pages, asking me questions... So I can't stop this. I don't even think I'd call it passion. It's pressure. It's a responsibility, and I can't stop. I won't.

Naomi: The time is passing quickly, and there is a moral responsibility to take care of this and to take care of it right. There is an incredible responsibility that comes with this. It's great just sitting here, writing checks all day long, but the responsibility that goes with it is pretty serious.

Terry: There's so much in life. There's so much beauty and so many marvelous aspects to life. They're coupled and balanced by those things that you may not think are so magical, but they're really one and the same. In order to have magic in your life, or a magical aspect in your life, it has to be balanced by that stuff that doesn't appear to be so magical but really is just as important.

Scotty: I propped up my body with my axe, tried to shake off the massive fatigue, and trudged on—step by step—up Mount Rainier. I was living out that choice again—the choice to keep going.

Gina: Accomplishment comes to me when I have finished a race, that overwhelming feeling of crossing a finish line. I created a blog, and I wanted to be an example to others that this was possible through hard work and the willingness to do it. I also run/ walk in many 5k races that give to a range of charities, and there is nothing better than that! I do approximately ten races a year.

Scotty: Every time I spoke, I healed. I would still get nervous in front of audiences I could not see, but I started to have a greater sense of purpose in my life as I interacted with others. My speeches—and my continued service on active duty—were giving others hope and helping the army in a small way. I felt like I was contributing again, rather than just taking from others.

Naomi: What you heard is the passion for what I do. It has become such an integral part of what I do—it has become such an integral part of me—that I cannot imagine my life not doing this... I don't think anything quite compares to what I do... I couldn't see not having a purposeful life like this. It's who I am... And it always gets paid forward. That is the beauty of it all.

Louise: I'm a facilitator. Ultimately, we all heal ourselves. Nobody can do it for us.

Scotty: As I worked and contributed, my life started to gain some meaning.

Terry: For me, hope has come from the knowledge that what I'm going through is supposed to be. And it's through that, because I continue to grow and learn that the future is not bleak for me, which is really what hope is about: hope is the desire, the wish, the prayer that everything's going to be okay. In my mind-set, everything already is okay.

Implementing Step 5: Take Authentic Action

You can only plan it for so long. Then it is time to do it.

The foundation of this step is Choice.

- Visualize your feet, knowing where to go, and walk in that direction.

- Do one thing today that takes you closer to where you want to be.

- Take a simple, authentic action today. Look at who benefits.

- Take a complex authentic action within the next week. Look at who benefits.

- What did you learn that you will not repeat on your next trip along the TransForMission Path?

- What are you most grateful for in Step 5?

One More Thing

For many years, I have lived as my dad suggested when he said, "You can do anything you set your mind to do." I still marvel at the gift he gave me with those words, even though our time together was short.

As I created the Path and followed my own TransForMission, I made a startling discovery:

My dad was wrong. It is not what is in my mind that makes me a transformed person. It is what is deep within me. I make the commitment to transform in my mind, but the truth of what I do comes from my heart.

If I had mentioned this in the introduction of the book, you might not have believed me. Now, at the end of our journey together, I know you will understand when I wish you *bon voyage* and tell you:

You can do anything you set your heart to do.

Happy New Year!

Acknowledgments

I am grateful for the friends and family who travel this path with me. They include Paulette Clements, Lisa Joiner, and Jenny Steinbeck, who provide valuable feedback; Debbi Horvath, who asks good questions; the Wednesday Women of Wisdom, who serve up large portions of support; Vicki Lorini, my buddy in CapRadio Reads; and the team at Balboa. Thanks to the folks from OHS, OU, KSU, ACE, TNS, SLC and CPR. I am grateful to Al Bartholet (even though neither of us knew he was helping until we both got there). Many thanks to the participants in TransForMission workshops for their help with the beta-testing of these concepts; I am honored to call you my buddies.

Big gratitude to the interviewees who generously shared intimate details of their experiences. Each conversation holds special meaning for me.

Special thanks to my first editors, Joe and Rita.

To all, I say,

Please and thank you.

CPSIA information can be obtained at www.ICGtesting.com
Printed in the USA
BVOW01*0702151014

370395BV00002B/2/P